ENGINEERING MARVELS

TUNNELS

Samantha S. Bell

Lightbox is an all-inclusive digital solution for the teaching and learning of curriculum topics in an original, groundbreaking way. Lightbox is based on National Curriculum Standards.

STANDARD FEATURES OF LIGHTBOX

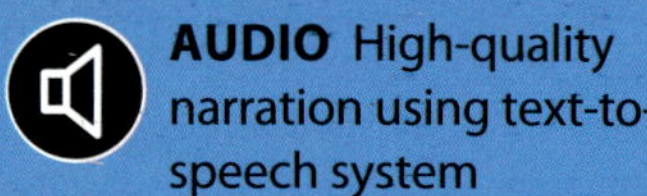
AUDIO High-quality narration using text-to-speech system

ACTIVITIES Printable PDFs that can be emailed and graded

SLIDESHOWS Pictorial overviews of key concepts

VIDEOS Embedded high-definition video clips

WEBLINKS Curated links to external, child-safe resources

TRANSPARENCIES Step-by-step layering of maps, diagrams, charts, and timelines

INTERACTIVE MAPS Interactive maps and aerial satellite imagery

QUIZZES Ten multiple choice questions that are automatically graded and emailed for teacher assessment

KEY WORDS Matching key concepts to their definitions

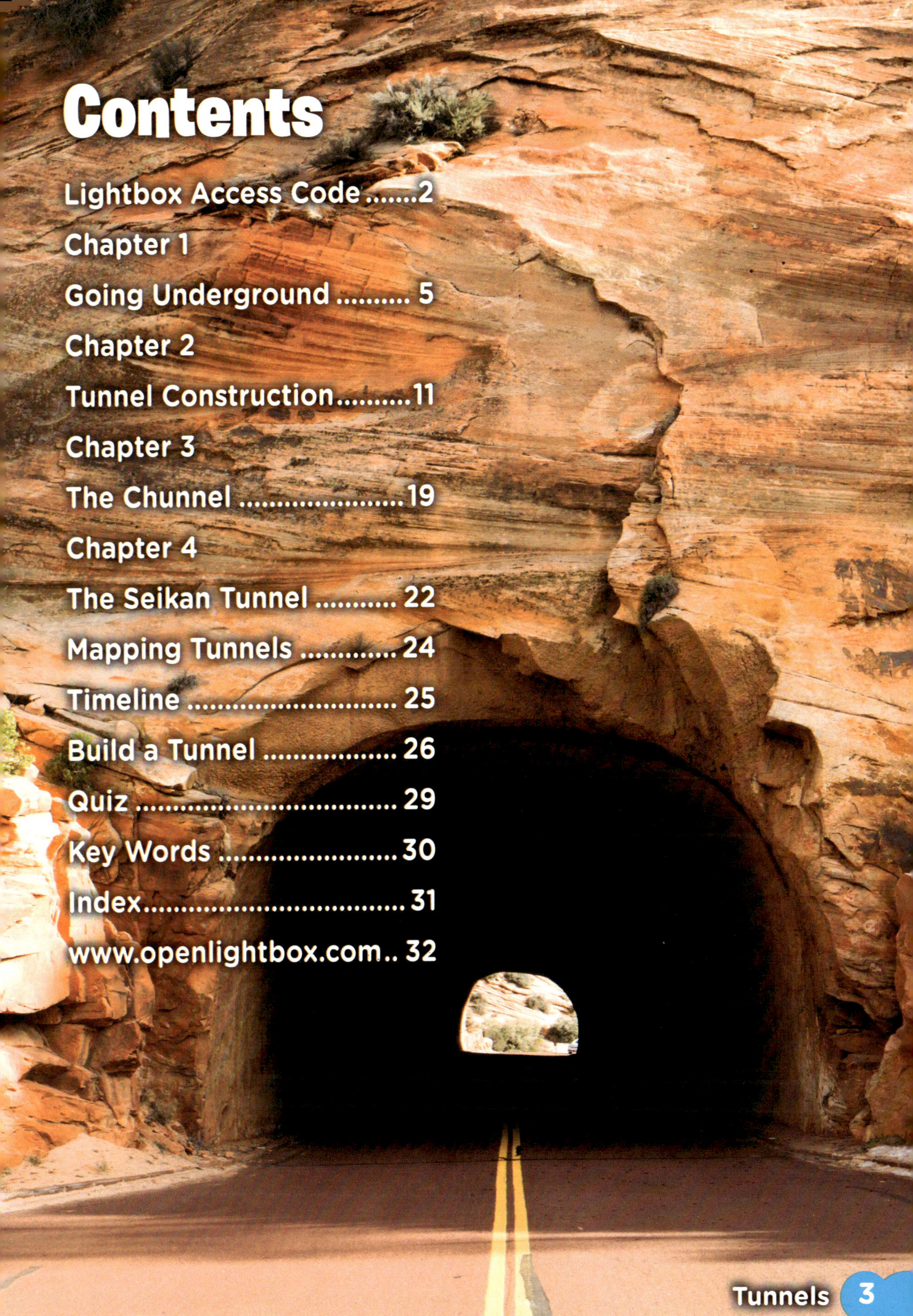

Contents

Lightbox Access Code 2
Chapter 1
Going Underground 5
Chapter 2
Tunnel Construction..........11
Chapter 3
The Chunnel 19
Chapter 4
The Seikan Tunnel 22
Mapping Tunnels 24
Timeline 25
Build a Tunnel 26
Quiz 29
Key Words 30
Index.................................. 31
www.openlightbox.com.. 32

Chapter 1

Going Underground

Anna smiled at her brother in the back seat. Their car was about to travel through the Laerdal Tunnel in Norway. It stretches 15.2 miles (24.5 kilometers). The drive from one side to the other takes more than 20 minutes. Engineers knew such a long drive in a dark tunnel could make people feel **claustrophobic** or tired.

It took five years to build the Laerdal Tunnel, which links Laerdal and Aurland, two cities in Norway.

For this reason, engineers designed **caverns** with colored lights. These caverns are every 3.7 miles (6.0 km). They are meant to help people stay alert. Suddenly, Anna's grandfather pulled into a parking bay, and the three got out of the car. They were standing under a mountain!

A tunnel is a long, narrow path under the ground. Tunnels are some of the most challenging projects in engineering and construction. Engineers spend a lot of time planning them. They must determine a **route**, study the ground, and design the **excavation** method and support. Years may pass between the idea of the tunnel and when construction begins.

People have been building tunnels for thousands of years. Ancient civilizations such as the Incas, Aztecs, Babylonians, and Egyptians all constructed tunnels. Engineers in ancient Rome built tunnels, too. The tunnels carried fresh water into the city and wastewater out.

Some of the earliest tunnels were built to hold or carry water, including Roman cisterns.

Israel's **Siloam Tunnel** is almost **3,000 years old**. It is one of the oldest tunnels that can still be visited today.

More than **25 miles** (40 km) of **tunnels** lie under the town of **Oppenheim**, Germany.

Many tunnels the **Romans** dug through **mountains 2,000 years ago** are still in use.

Tunnels can significantly cut down travel times from one place to another.

For hundreds of years, people built tunnels using simple tools. They used hammers and **chisels** to break through rock. Technology for tunnel building did not change much until the 1600s. That's when workers started blasting away the rock with gunpowder. They later used dynamite.

With the development of trains in the 1800s, engineers began building more tunnels to make travel easier. In the 1950s, tunnel-**boring** machines (TBMs) first were used. These machines could do the job much faster than dynamite.

Today, engineers create tunnels beneath cities, through mountains, and even under the ocean. Modern technology has made it possible to build tunnels in places that used to be **impassable**. Tunnels carry water, sewage, power lines, and communication lines. Tunnels also carry people. They are a way to connect cities, states, and even countries.

Chapter 2

Tunnel Construction

Before building a tunnel, engineers spend a lot of time planning. They study the ground to learn how it might act during construction. Engineers also study the site conditions and make sure codes are followed. Codes are safety requirements set by the government.

In the United States, at least 15 cities have subway systems.

Engineers then recommend how to build the tunnel. The goal is to build the highest quality tunnel within budget. Engineers decide what support will be needed. They make sure the project is safe for the workers. They also consider how the tunnel will affect other things in that location. For example, tunnels could disrupt wildlife and the natural environment.

A tunnel's arched roof supports the weight of the ground above it better than a flat roof.

In addition, engineers think about the people who will use the tunnel. If the tunnel is a roadway, it must have enough lights for safe travel. Long tunnels also need good **ventilation systems**. These provide fresh air and remove **exhaust**. Tunnels must also have a way for people to escape if there is a problem.

All tunnels need to be designed to withstand the weight of the surrounding material. The ground pushes down, and the weight arches around the tunnel.

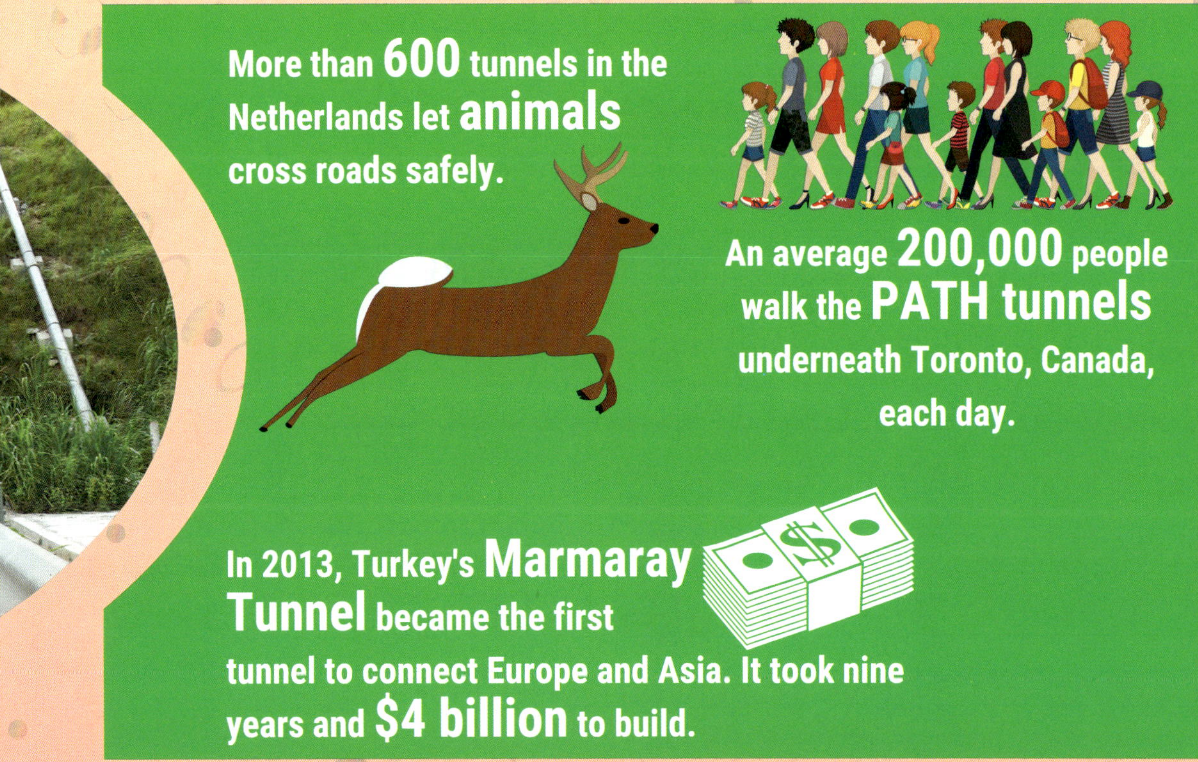

Depending on the strength of the ground, a support system may be installed. Strong materials help support the tunnel.

Tunnels are constructed in different ways. Soft-ground tunnels are built where the ground is made of soil. If the tunnel is not too deep, workers typically use the cut-and-cover method to build the tunnel. They dig a trench and build the tunnel structure in sections. Then they cover it. Subways, water supply systems, and sewer systems are often associated with soft-ground tunnels.

Rock tunnels are built through mountains or other rocky landforms. They provide faster routes for cars or trains. Workers used to make rock tunnels by blasting the mountains with dynamite. Today, huge TBMs offer another option to chew through the rock.

TBMs have rotating cutters that chew through rock.

Underwater tunnels allow travel under the sea. Some are dug under the ocean floor. Workers often build these tunnels in sections. Then they dig a trench in the sea floor. They float all of the sections into place and sink them. Divers attach the sections together.

A TBM can typically dig 50 to 60 feet (15 to 18 meters) of tunnel a day.

Engineering Design Process

Engineers use various tools and do many tests in their planning. Once a tunnel is built, they expect the design to be safe and sturdy.

ASK What will the tunnel be used for? What kind of ground will the tunnel go through? What equipment is needed to build the tunnel? How can the effects on the environment be limited? What safety precautions should be made?

IMAGINE Brainstorm possible ways to build the tunnel. What excavation method would work best?

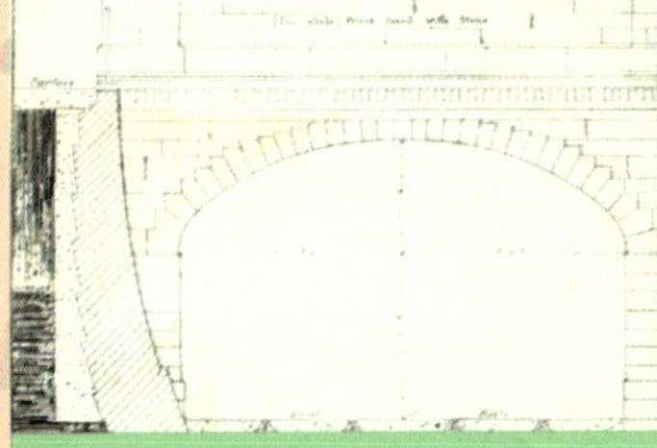

PLAN Draw a diagram of the tunnel. Make a list of materials needed. Write down a list of steps.

CREATE Follow the plan and build the tunnel.

IMPROVE What worked with the tunnel? What did not work? Change the design to make the tunnel better. Test it.

Chapter 3

The Chunnel

The English Channel separates England and France. In the past, travelers had to cross it by **ferry**. This took 45 minutes. Today, a train going through the Chunnel can reach the other side in 20 minutes. The Chunnel is 31 miles (50 km) long. Approximately 23 miles (37 km) of this tunnel are underwater.

Up to 400 trains pass through the Chunnel every day.

Planners needed to make sure the Chunnel was safe. So they built three tunnels instead of one. A service tunnel runs between two train tunnels. It acts as an escape route in case of a fire. Engineers also created passages every 410 yards (375 m). These allow the trains to switch tracks if necessary.

Construction began in 1988. More than 13,000 people from France and England worked on the Chunnel. They used TBMs to chew through a layer of chalky ground 130 feet (40 m) under the ocean floor. Many of the machines were as long as two football fields. It took three years for the machines to dig all the way through. The tunnel was then lined with concrete and cast iron rings.

One year after the Chunnel opened, a fire broke out on a train. Thirty-one people were on the train. They all escaped through the service tunnel. Fires also broke out in 2008 and 2015, but no one was seriously injured.

To use the Chunnel, cars are put on a special train called the Eurotunnel Car Transporter.

Chapter 4

The Seikan Tunnel

In 1954, a typhoon sank five ferries on the Tsugaru **Strait** in Japan. More than 1,000 people died. Engineers worked to create a safer crossing. In 1964, construction finally began on the Seikan Tunnel, the world's longest and deepest underwater tunnel.

The Seikan Tunnel cost as much as $7 billion to build.

The ground under the strait was unpredictable. This made the work difficult and slow. Instead of using a TBM, workers had to drill and blast through the earth. They went right through a major fault zone. The tunnel was finished in 1988. More than 14 miles (23 km) of the tunnel's 33 miles (53 km) are under the Tsugaru Strait.

Mapping Tunnels

Although the United States is not home to the longest tunnels in the world, it does have many notable, important, and beautiful ones. The map shows where some of these engineering marvels are found around the country. Which is the closest tunnel to you?

1

Lincoln Tunnel

New York and New Jersey

Length: 1.5 miles (2.4 km)

The Lincoln Tunnel connects New York City with New Jersey. It is one of the busiest road tunnels in the United States. An average of 110,000 vehicles pass through it every day.

2

Eisenhower Tunnel

Dillon, Colorado

Length: 1.7 miles (2.7 km)

The Eisenhower Tunnel in the Rocky Mountains is one of the highest tunnels in the world, at an elevation of 11,158 feet (3,401 m). It passes through the Continental Divide of the United States.

3

Zion-Mount Carmel Tunnel

Springdale, Utah

Length: 1.1 miles (1.8 km)

The Zion-Mount Carmel Tunnel in Utah connects Mount Zion National Park to Bryce Canyon National Park. It has windows carved into its sides so drivers can take in the majestic views.

UNITED STATES

Atlantic Ocean

Pacific Ocean

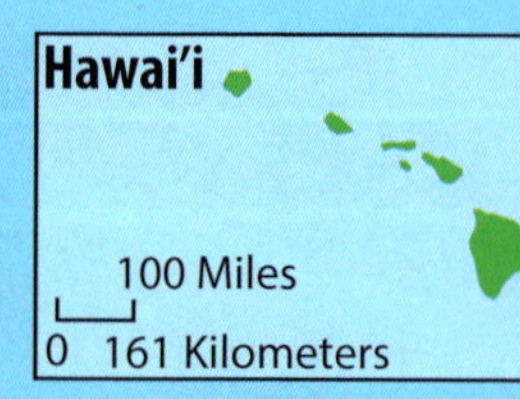

Legend

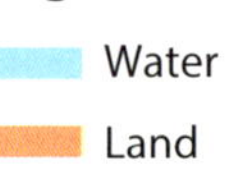

250 Miles
0 402 Kilometers

Timeline

Tunnels allow people to travel quickly from destination to destination. They cut through obstacles or allow people to travel underground. Discover more about the history of tunnels in the United States.

1875

The Hoosac Tunnel in Massachusetts is completed. It is one of the first tunnels to be made using dynamite.

1897

The first trains start running in the Boston Subway. It is the first subway system built in the United States.

1904

The New York City Subway opens. In the last century, it has grown to be the busiest U.S. subway system, with almost 6 million riders a day.

1936

The Yerba Buena Tunnel in California is completed. It is the world's widest single-bore tunnel. Today, there are five lanes of traffic that pass through the tunnel.

2000

Started in the early 1900s, the Anton Anderson Memorial Tunnel in Alaska is completed. At 2.5 miles (4 km) long, it is the longest tunnel in North America, and makes both train and vehicle travel possible.

2017

Big Bertha, the world's largest TBM, completes a 1.7-mile (2.7-km) tunnel in Seattle, Washington.

Build a Tunnel

Now it is your turn to build a tunnel through a clay mountain. Can you dig a tunnel through the mountain without it cracking?

Materials

You will need modeling clay, a spoon, and a toilet paper tube. Also find two or three items with long, thick handles.

Procedure

1. Find a good place to work, such as a table. If needed, you can use a large piece of waxed paper or cardboard to keep your work space clean.
2. Place the modeling clay on the work surface. The clay should be in a big mound, like a mountain.
3. Create a tunnel by digging. Use the spoon to dig a tunnel all the way through the mountain.
4. Next, build a tunnel by boring. Reshape the clay back into a mountain. Then choose an object with a thick, long handle, such as a hairbrush or ladle.

5. Place the end of the handle against the side of the mountain. To create the tunnel, push the handle through the clay until it comes out the other side.

Improve It!

Your clay mountain might have cracked when you pushed the handle through. How can you change your process to avoid cracking?

Tunnel-boring machines spin as they cut through rock and clay. What do you think will happen if you rotate the handle as you push it? Try it to find out.

Linings help support tunnels. How can you use the toilet paper tube to give your tunnel more support?

Engineers have to choose the right equipment for the job. Try using different objects to bore through the tunnel, such as a marker, a ruler, or even your fingers. Which ones work the best?

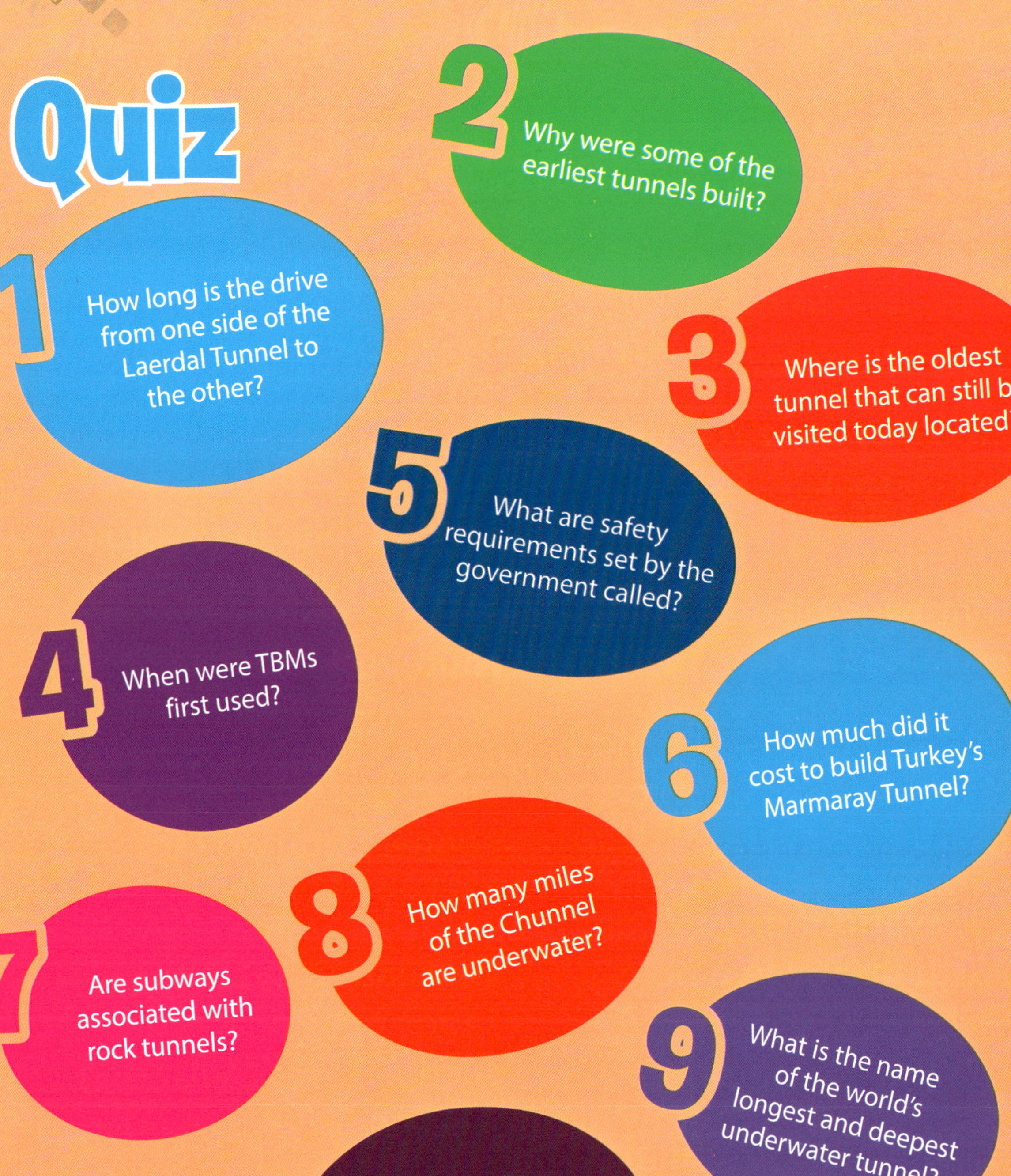

Answers

1. Twenty minutes **2.** To hold or carry water **3.** Israel **4.** The 1950s **5.** Codes
6. $4 billion **7.** No, with soft-ground tunnels **8.** 23 miles (37 km)
9. Seikan Tunnel **10.** 2017

Key Words

boring: making a hole by digging away material

caverns: large rooms dug out in rock

chisels: metal tools that have blades with cutting edges

claustrophobic: having a fear of being in narrow or closed-in spaces

excavation: digging out earth to create a hole or tunnel

exhaust: the gas that escapes from an engine

ferry: a boat used to move people, vehicles, or goods from one place to another

impassable: impossible to get across or travel over

route: a path or a specific way to get somewhere

strait: a narrow waterway connecting two large bodies of water

ventilation systems: a series of connected parts, such as fans, that bring in fresh air and remove stale air

Index

Aztecs 6

Babylonians 6

Chunnel 19, 20, 21, 29
communication lines 9
cut-and-cover 14

dynamite 8, 9, 14, 25

Egyptians 6
England 19, 20
environment 12, 17
excavation 6, 17

France 19, 20

Incas 6

Japan 22

Laerdal Tunnel 5, 29

materials 14, 17

Norway 5

Rome 6

Seikan Tunnel 22, 29
sewers 14
subways 14, 29

tunnel-boring machines
(TBMs) 9, 14, 15, 16, 20,
23, 25, 29

underwater tunnels 16, 19, 20

water supply systems 7, 9, 14

LIGHTBOX

SUPPLEMENTARY RESOURCES

Click on the plus icon found in the bottom left corner of each spread to open additional teacher resources.

- Download and print the book's quizzes and activities
- Access curriculum correlations
- Explore additional web applications that enhance the Lightbox experience

LIGHTBOX DIGITAL TITLES

Packed full of integrated media

VIDEOS

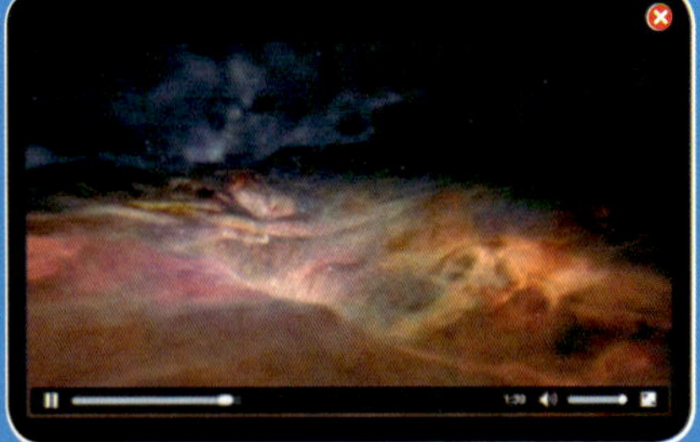

INTERACTIVE MAPS

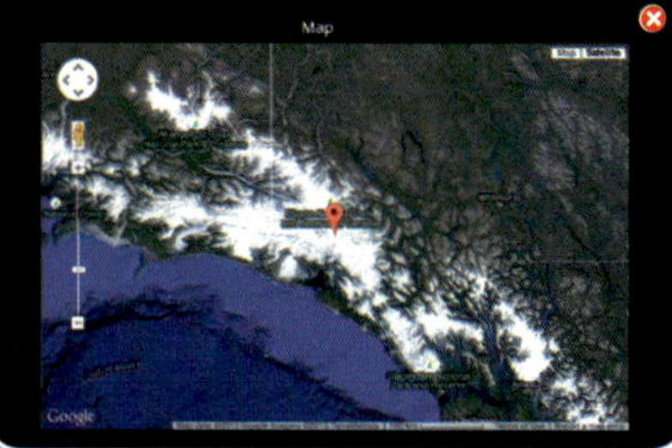

WEBLINKS

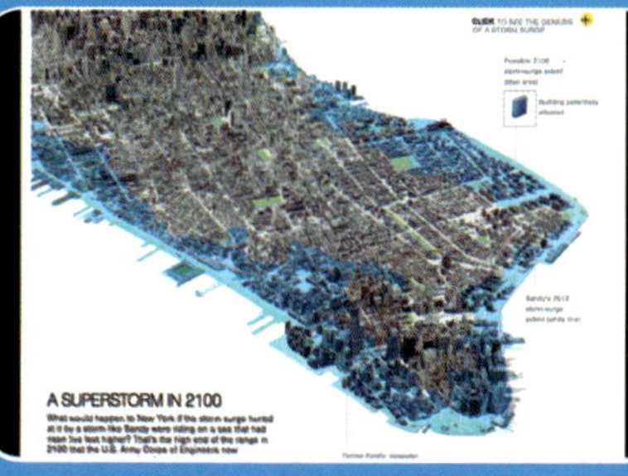

SLIDESHOWS

QUIZZES

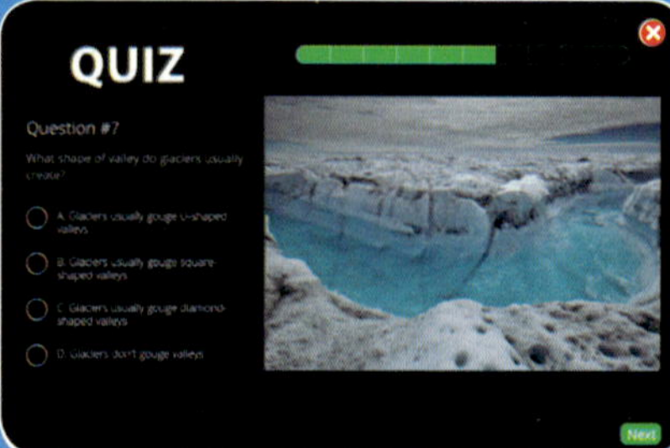

OPTIMIZED FOR

- ✔ TABLETS
- ✔ WHITEBOARDS
- ✔ COMPUTERS
- ✔ AND MUCH MORE!

Published by Smartbook Media Inc.
350 5th Avenue, 59th Floor New York, NY 10118
Website: www.openlightbox.com

012018
151217

Library of Congress Control Number: 2017961996

ISBN 978-1-5105-3740-8 (hardcover)
ISBN 978-1-5105-3741-5 (multi-user eBook)

Printed in the Brainerd, Minnesota, United States
1 2 3 4 5 6 7 8 9 0 22 21 20 19 18

First published by North Star Editions in 2018.

Project Coordinator: Jared Siemens
Designer: Ana María Vidal

Every reasonable effort has been made to trace ownership and to obtain permission to reprint copyright material. The publisher would be pleased to have any errors or omissions brought to its attention so that they may be corrected in subsequent printings.

The publisher acknowledges Alamy, Getty Images, iStock, and Shutterstock as the primary image suppliers for this title.